Travel Guide To Segovia 2023

Unveiling the Historic Marvels: A Journey through Segovia's Timeless Beauty

Timothy S. Govea

Table Of Contents

INTRODUCTION

Welcome to Segovia

Welcome to Segovia, a city dripping with timeless beauty and history. Segovia, a charming city in the centre of Spain, will take you back in time with its preserved architectural wonders and extensive cultural history.

Segovia has much to offer for everyone, regardless of your interests in history, food, or adventure. The city is full of breathtaking attractions just waiting to be discovered, like the landmark Aqueduct of Segovia, a monument to ancient engineering, and the grandiose Alcázar of Segovia, a fairytale-like stronghold located on a mountaintop.

This travel book will be your dependable travel companion as you set out on your excursion through Segovia, giving you in-depth knowledge, insider advice, and suggested itineraries to help you make the most of your stay. Make lifelong memories while exploring the city's hidden beauties, indulging in local food, and becoming fully immersed in the community.

Whether you visit Segovia for a brief visit or a lengthy journey, it will have a lasting impression on you. Pack your bags, prepare your mind, and get ready to discover Segovia, Spain's timeless beauty, and its historic wonders. Start your exploration now!

GETTING TO KNOW SEGOVIA

Overview of Segovia

Segovia, a historic city in the centre of Spain, is well-known for its magnificent architecture and cultural value. With a population of about 55,000, Segovia has a small-town charm that attracts tourists from all over the world.

- The city has a long history, with signs of settlement dating back to the Bronze Age. The beautiful Segovia Aqueduct was built during the Roman Empire, nevertheless, and this is when Segovia had its greatest prosperity.

  One of Segovia's most recognizable structures, this spectacular building dates back to the first century AD and serves as a reminder of the Romans' highly developed engineering capabilities.

- The Alcázar of Segovia, a fairytale-like stronghold located atop a rocky outcrop, is another well-known site in Segovia. This majestic castle, with its recognizable turrets and breathtaking views of the surrounding countryside, holds an important place in Spanish history and represents the magnificence of the city.

- The well-preserved mediaeval structures and meandering lanes that characterise Segovia's old centre make it a UNESCO World Heritage Site. Visitors can take in the city's rich cultural past while exploring the Jewish Quarter (La Judera) or the scenic Plaza Mayor. They can also find quaint stores, cafés, and restaurants.

- Additionally, the city is home to numerous museums and galleries that display a wide variety of creative and historical treasures. For culture vultures of all ages, Segovia offers an immersive cultural experience with Roman relics, mediaeval art, and modern exhibitions.

- Segovia is surrounded by breathtaking natural beauty in addition to its historical and cultural attractions. The city is tucked between the Eresma and Clamores rivers, and the Guadarrama Mountains, and offers stunning scenery as well as chances for outdoor pursuits including hiking, nature walks, and exploring adjacent natural parks.

Segovia is a place that captures the hearts of those who visit because of its rich history, architectural marvels, cultural vibrancy, and natural appeal. Segovia guarantees a unique experience for every visitor, regardless of whether they are drawn to Gothic churches, traditional food, or the serene beauty of the countryside.

Segovia's History and Culture

The long history of Segovia has left behind a rich tapestry of civilizations that have shaped the city's culture and character. Segovia's historical and cultural history is amazing, spanning from prehistoric settlements to Roman domination, majestic mediaeval architecture, and contemporary construction.

- The city's history may be traced back to prehistoric times, and Bronze Age human habitation is suggested by archaeological findings. Segovia thrived as a significant urban centre, nonetheless, during the Roman era. The Segovia Aqueduct, a feat of engineering that originally provided water to the city, is the most recognizable reminder of Roman influence in Segovia.

The aqueduct is a striking example of Roman architecture, with imposing arches that span more than 800 metres.

- Segovia was ruled by the Visigoths and the Moors several times after the Roman Empire's fall. However, the city's greatest age of cultural and architectural development occurred during the Middle Ages. During this time, the beautiful Alcázar of Segovia, a fortress that combines Moorish and Gothic characteristics, was built. The

Segovia Cathedral, a massive Gothic building with exquisite workmanship, came to represent the city's importance in both religion and the arts.

- The Judera, or Jewish community, of Segovia, flourished in the Middle Ages. With its winding lanes and ancient structures, Segovia's Jewish Quarter offers a glimpse into the thriving Jewish community that once presided there.

- Segovia has a long history of serving as a hub for artistic and academic endeavours. Renowned poets, authors, and painters who have contributed to the cultural legacy of the city have called it home. The city's cultural sector is still thriving today, with many festivals, concerts, and exhibitions happening all year long.

- The culture of Segovia also includes cuisine. The region is renowned for its regional cuisine, which includes roast lamb and cochinillo (suckling pig). Visitors can enjoy the tastes and culinary customs that have been passed down through the generations by learning about the local cuisine.

- Segovia's selection as a UNESCO World Heritage Site is proof that its historical and cultural significance is acknowledged on a global scale. Visitors are captivated by the city's well-preserved architecture, historic landmarks, and rich cultural traditions because they offer a singular and immersive glimpse into the past.

Segovia's history and culture are intricately woven together, creating a mesmerising tapestry that beckons tourists to dig into its timeless beauty, whether they choose to see the Roman aqueduct, stroll through mediaeval alleyways, or indulge in local cuisine.

Geography and Climate

About 90 kilometres (56 miles) north of Madrid, the country's capital, Segovia is located in the country's centre region. The city is tucked away in the Sierra de Guadarrama mountain range's foothills, which is a part of the Central System.

- Rolling hills, vast plains, and stunning valleys make up the region that surrounds Segovia. The region's natural beauty is enhanced by the flow of the Eresma and Clamores rivers.

- Segovia has a continental climate with scorching summers and chilly winters because of its location in the interior. The many seasons are broken down below along with some general descriptions of each:

- **Spring (March to May)**: Segovia experiences pleasant springtime temperatures with daily highs averaging between 13°C (55°F) and 20°C (68°F). It's a lovely time to go because nature is in full bloom with blooming flowers and lush vegetation.

- **Summer (June to August)**: Segovia's summers can be hot, with average highs of 30°C (86°F) and lows of 25°C (77°F). The warmest months, with occasional heatwaves, are July and August. While exploring the city during this period, it is advised to bring sunscreen, wear hats, and drink enough water.

- **Autumn (September to November):** Segovia's autumn is moderate and enjoyable, with temperatures that gradually drop. With average highs between 17°C (63°F) and 25°C (77°F), autumn is the perfect time to engage in outdoor activities and take in the changing leaves.

- **Winter (December to February):** Segovia's winters can be chilly, with daily highs and lows between 3°C (37°F) and 10°C (50°F). Snowfall is frequent at this time of year, giving the city's landmarks a surreal appearance. It is important to wear warm clothing and be ready for cool weather.

- Throughout the year, Segovia receives a modest amount of precipitation, with the spring and fall months seeing significantly more. When travelling during these seasons, it is important to have an umbrella or raincoat with you.

Because of its mountainous surroundings and natural parks, the city is ideally situated for outdoor pursuits including hiking, nature hikes, and visiting the picturesque countryside.

Visitors can make the most of the region's various seasons and natural beauty by planning their excursions appropriately, packing the right attire, and being aware of the topography and climate of Segovia.

PLANNING YOUR TRIP

Best Time to Visit Segovia

Depending on your preferences and the kind of experience you're looking for, there is no one optimum time to visit Segovia. Here is a list of the many seasons and what they have to offer:

1. **Spring (March to May):** Segovia is a wonderful place to visit in the springtime. The weather is nice, and the temperature is rising gradually. Flowers are in bloom, the scenery is lush and green, and the weather is pleasant for visiting the city's attractions.

   It's a great time to go sightseeing, engage in outdoor activities, and take in Segovia's stunning scenery.

2. **Summer (June to August):** Segovia can experience scorching summers with sporadic high temperatures. But if you don't mind the heat, this time of year can be a fantastic time to travel. Longer daylight hours throughout the summer give you more time to visit the city's landmarks.

Consider scheduling your activities for the mornings or evenings when it is a little cooler and be prepared for warmer temperatures.

3. **Autumn (September to November):** If you like more moderate weather and fewer tourists, autumn is a great season to visit Segovia. With colder temperatures and lovely autumn foliage, the weather is nice. It's a wonderful time to engage in outdoor pursuits like hiking or strolls in the city

parks while taking in the stunning fall scenery.

4. **Winter (December to February):** Segovia experiences cooler temperatures and sporadic snowfall during the winter, which can give the city's landmarks a pleasant finishing touch.

This can be a fantastic time to travel if you like the winter scenery and fewer visitors. Just be ready for the cold and wear warm clothing. It's important to keep in mind that some attractions may have fewer hours of operation in the winter.

It's crucial to organise your visit taking into account the preferred weather, availability, and your intended activities. Remember that spring and autumn typically provide more comfortable weather and conducive conditions for exploration. However, you may still take in Segovia's beauty during those seasons provided you're prepared for the sweltering heat of summer or the bitter cold of winter.

Additionally, it's a good idea to look into the regional celebrations and events that Segovia has throughout the year since these can enrich your trip with a distinctive cultural experience.

Duration of Stay

Depending on your interests, available time, and desired level of exploration, the perfect length of stay in Segovia can change. The following elements should be taken into account while choosing the length of your visit:

1. Segovia's principal attractions, including the Jewish Quarter, the Alcázar of Segovia, the Segovia Cathedral, and the Segovia Aqueduct, can all be toured in a day or two. If you only have a short amount of time and want to concentrate on the city's highlights, a one- to two-day visit would be sufficient.

2. **Cultural Experiences:** Think about extending your stay by three or four days if you want to fully experience the local culture, visit museums and art galleries, go to festivals, or learn more about Segovia's history and traditions. You'll have more time as a result to take advantage of the city's cultural offers and engage in other activities.

3. **Day visits:** Segovia is a great starting point for day visits to neighbouring places because of its advantageous

position. It's suggested to allot extra time for these trips if you intend to explore the neighbourhood and stop by attractions like the Royal Palace of La Granja de San Ildefonso or the local parks. Day trips can be added to your itinerary if you are staying for four to five days or longer.

4. Consider extending your stay beyond a few days if you prefer a laid-back and leisurely visit that gives you enough opportunity to meander through the streets, eat local cuisine, and take in Segovia's atmosphere. You'll be able to take breaks, find hidden jewels, and enjoy the charm of the city at a more leisurely pace as a result of this.

The length of your visit to Segovia ultimately relies on your particular tastes and the activities you want to partake in. Planning your itinerary is advised. Consider the places you want to see, any day trips you want to do, and the kind of experience you want to have all together. Whatever the length of your stay, Segovia's fascinating architecture, rich history, and cultural attractions are sure to leave a lasting impact.

Travel Essentials and Tips

It's critical to plan and bring the appropriate travel necessities when visiting Segovia. Here are some suggestions for your trip, including goods to pack:

1. **Clothing for the Weather**: Bring clothes appropriate for the season and predicted weather. Layers are a must because temperatures can change during the day. The best way to explore

Segovia's historic centre is on foot, so don't forget to bring some comfy walking shoes.

2. **Travel Documents**: Bring your passport or other form of photo identification, as well as any other necessary travel papers, like a visa or proof of travel insurance. Physical copies and digital backups should both be kept in a secure location.

3. Although credit cards are frequently used, it is still a good idea to carry some local currency with you in case you need to make a minor transaction or visit a place that doesn't accept cards. There are ATMs located all over the city where you can get cash.

4. **Voltage and Adapters**: If you're coming from a location with a different plug type or voltage, think about packing a

universal adapter to make sure you can charge your electronic gadgets. The common voltage in Spain is 230V, and the plugs are of the Europlug variety (two round pins).

5. Although English is widely spoken in Segovia, it still helps to know a few basic Spanish words or have a phrasebook for everyday conversations. The effort to converse in their tongue is frequently appreciated by the locals.

6. Segovia is a relatively safe city, although it's always advisable to use caution and pay attention to your surroundings. Take the required security measures to safeguard your possessions, and stay away from showcasing priceless objects in crowded places. Additionally, it is

advised to have emergency phone numbers around.

7. Learn how to use public transit to navigate around Segovia and to neighbouring attractions by becoming familiar with the available alternatives, which include buses and trains. To make the most of your time, review timetables and make appropriate plans.

8. **Sun protection**: Segovia can experience intense sun exposure, particularly in the summer. To shield yourself from UV rays, bring sunscreen, sunglasses, and a hat.

9. Consider purchasing travel insurance to protect against unforeseen circumstances like medical emergencies, trip cancellations, or misplaced luggage. Check the policy's

specifics to make sure they satisfy your unique demands.

10. **Investigate Off-Peak Hours:** If you want to see popular attractions without crowds, think about going early in the morning or late in the day. Better photo chances and a more enjoyable experience are made possible as a result.

To guarantee a smooth and comfortable stay, don't forget to read the most recent travel warnings and instructions before your trip. You can make the most of your stay in Segovia and create priceless memories by being organised and keeping in mind these packing requirements and travel advice.

Budgeting and Currency

Budgeting for your trip to Segovia and familiarising yourself with the local currency are crucial. Here are some suggestions for managing your finances and currency:

1. **Currency**: The Euro (€) is Spain's official unit of exchange. It is essential to exchange some money before your journey or to use an ATM when you get to Segovia to get cash. Major credit cards are accepted at the majority of places, and ATMs are widely dispersed around the city.

2. **Exchange Rates:** To estimate how much your currency is worth in euros, keep an eye on the current exchange rates. Before converting any currencies, it is a good idea to check with reputable sources or speak with your bank because exchange rates might vary.

3. Establish your travel budget, taking into account the cost of lodging, meals, transportation, sightseeing, and any additional activities or shopping you intend to do. To determine how much to set aside for each category, look up the average expenditures of various expenses in Segovia.

4. **Accommodations**: Segovia offers a range of lodging alternatives, from high-end hotels to inexpensive hostels. When deciding on the kind of lodging that best matches your needs, take into account your tastes and budget. Booking in advance or choosing off-peak times can frequently result in lower pricing.

5. **Dining**: To accommodate a variety of budgets, Segovia offers a variety of dining alternatives. There are many

options, ranging from fancy restaurants to neighbourhood cafés and tapas bars. The "menu of the day," which frequently offers a fixed-price meal with numerous courses at a reasonable price, is a good option for affordable meals.

6. **Travel**: Segovia's small size makes it simple to explore on foot, especially in the old centre. However, plan for the cost of bus or train fare if you intend to visit neighbouring sites or if you want to take public transit. Public transportation in Segovia is generally inexpensive and effective.

7. Attractions and entrance fees: Segovia's attractions may charge an entrance fee. Consider the expenditures in your budget after doing some preliminary research. Inquire about any discounts that might

be offered since many attractions provide reduced prices for visitors who are young, old, or with families.

8. **Shopping and Souvenirs**: Set aside a portion of your budget for these costs if you intend to go shopping or buy souvenirs. You can find regional arts, delicacies, and traditional goods in Segovia's many stores, markets, and boutiques.

9. **Service fees and gratuities**: In Spain, gratuities are not as commonplace as they are in some other nations. However, it's customary to round up the total or add a little tip (often between 5 and 10 percent) for excellent service received at restaurants, from tour guides, or hotel staff.

You can manage your costs wisely and have fun in Segovia without worrying about money if you take this budgeting advice into account and have a solid grasp of the local currency.

EXPLORING SEGOVIA

The Aqueduct of Segovia

One of the most recognizable and impressive Roman buildings in the entire world is the Aqueduct of Segovia. This historic aqueduct, which spans more than 800 metres (2,600 feet) and rises to a height of 28 metres (92 feet), is a work of engineering genius and a reminder of the Roman civilization's inventiveness.

1. The aqueduct was built beginning in the first century AD under the rule of Emperor Domitian, and it was finished in the second century AD.

   Water was brought to Segovia via the aqueduct from the close-by Sierra de Guadarrama mountains, assuring a steady water supply for the city's citizens.

2. More than 20,000 granite blocks, each skillfully laid without the aid of mortar, make up the aqueduct. Given the structure's age, the construction's accuracy and stability are astounding.

3. The aqueduct is made up of two levels of arches: the top level has 44 smaller arches and the lower level has 75 semicircular arches. To ensure stability over the unsteady ground, the arches were built to spread the weight of the water.

4. In the centre of the city is where the Segovia Aqueduct's most well-known part may be found. The aqueduct here spans Plaza del Azoguejo, producing a stunning scene that enthrals tourists. A very impressive sight is the grandeur and sheer size of the aqueduct set

against the backdrop of Segovia's historic structures.

5. The Segovia Aqueduct, which was named a UNESCO World Heritage Site in 1985, is a magnificent illustration of Roman engineering and architectural skill. It continues to be a representation of Segovia's cultural legacy and acts as a potent reminder of the city's long history.

6. The splendour of the aqueduct can be appreciated by visitors who wander along it or who see it from various locations throughout the city. The aqueduct is especially beautiful at sunset or when lit up at night, when a magnificent ambiance is created.

For everyone visiting the city, the Segovia Aqueduct is a must-see destination. It offers an amazing look at the Romans' engineering prowess and a connection to Segovia's past that is both inspiring and humbling.

Alcázar of Segovia

The beautiful Alcázar of Segovia is perched stoically atop a rocky ledge overlooking the city. The Alcázar is one of Spain's most well-known sights due to its fairytale-like appearance and distinctive fusion of architectural elements.

- The Alcázar's beginnings can be found in the 12th century when it was used as a fortification. It received numerous upgrades and additions over the years, resulting in the spectacular building we see today.

  Moorish, Gothic, and Romanesque characteristics may all be seen in the architecture, which reflects a variety of influences.

- The Alcázar's exterior is appealing. Awe and astonishment are evoked by its towering towers, beautifully carved façades, and breathtaking vistas of the surroundings. The prow of a ship is frequently used to describe the castle's silhouette against the sky, giving it a special and distinctive profile.

- Visitors are welcome to tour the Alcázar's ornately furnished halls, chapels, and rooms. Highlights include the Royal Throne Room, which has superb tapestries and royal portraits, and the Hall of the Kings, which has an outstanding oak ceiling covered in coats of arms.

The museum of the castle displays a variety of old objects from its illustrious past, including armour, weapons, and works of art.

- The Tower of Juan II, which provides sweeping views of Segovia and the surrounding countryside, is one of Alcázar's most well-known features. Visitors who ascend the tower are rewarded with spectacular panoramas that go as far as the eye can see.

- In Spanish history, the Alcázar of Segovia has had a considerable impact. It was used as a state jail, a royal castle, and even the model for Walt Disney's Cinderella Castle.

  Due to its grandeur and historical significance, it is a well-liked tourist attraction and a must-visit location for people who enjoy history, architecture, and fairy tales.

The Alcázar of Segovia is a magnificent castle with a scenic site, intricate architectural features, and interesting interiors. The Alcázar captures the magic and fascination of Segovia's ageless charm, whether you explore its rooms, take in the panoramic vistas, or just awe at its outside beauty.

Jewish Quarter (La Judería)

Segovia's "La Judera," or Jewish Quarter, is a fascinating area that provides a window into the city's Jewish history and the vibrant life that formerly flourished there. This historic district, which is close to the city centre, is a reminder of Segovia's multiethnic past.

- Segovia was home to a thriving Jewish community during the Middle Ages.

The centre of this neighbourhood, La Judera, was where Jewish folks resided, went to work, and attended services. The quarter has kept its winding lanes, well-preserved structures, and architectural relics from its illustrious past.

- Visitors can fully experience La Judera's distinctive atmosphere by exploring the area. Architectural gems like the Casa de Abraham Seneor, a prominent Jewish house, and the Synagogue of El Transito.

A mediaeval synagogue that has been transformed into a museum displaying Sephardic Jewish culture and history, may be found as you stroll along its cobblestone streets.

- Another important site that illustrates the community's presence in Segovia is the Jewish Cemetery, which is close to La Judera. It serves as a reminder of the long-lasting Jewish presence in the city, despite being largely in ruins.

- La Judera is now a bustling neighbourhood in Segovia with quaint stores, eateries, and art galleries. It offers a distinctive setting where guests may immerse themselves in the history of the region, discover undiscovered nooks, and discover the cultural and religious contributions of the Jewish population.

As you go through La Judera, you'll see wonderfully preserved buildings with Hebrew inscriptions and have a chance to recreate the lively streets where Jewish families, craftspeople, and merchants used to go about their everyday lives.

A trip to Segovia's Jewish Quarter offers a chance to consider the historical significance of the Jewish population to the city as well as a fuller knowledge of Segovia's eclectic past. It's an opportunity to recognize the historical contributions made by the diverse cultural influences that have created Segovia's identity.

Plaza Mayor

Segovia's main square, Plaza Mayor, is a hive of activity, a place for social meetings and for cultural events. It is a well-liked gathering spot for both locals and guests given its central location.

- The square has its roots in the mediaeval times, when it was a marketplace and a hub of civic activity. Plaza Mayor has maintained its relevance as a hub of Segovian culture and community over the years.

- The area, which is surrounded by magnificent buildings, displays a fusion of Gothic, Renaissance, and Baroque architectural styles. The elaborate features, opulent balconies, and attractive arcades on the building facades serve as a magnificent backdrop to the lively environment.

- Plaza Mayor serves as a location for a wide range of events and celebrations in addition to being a stunning architectural landmark. Concerts, traditional performances, cultural exhibitions, and seasonal fairs animate the square all year round.

Plaza Mayor offers a wide variety of events for guests to enjoy, from exciting music festivals to the bustling Christmas market.

- The square is a great place to unwind and indulge in regional cuisine because it also has a variety of stores, cafés, and restaurants. You can enjoy a cup of coffee or try some local specialties while soaking up the vibrant atmosphere and taking in the busy activities all around you.

- The Plaza Mayor is a fantastic place to start your exploration of Segovia. From here, it's simple to reach other well-known sights including the Cathedral, the Alcázar, and the streets of the old city.

Experiencing Segovia's energy, taking in the architectural charm of the city, and immersing oneself in its dynamic social and cultural scene are all made possible by visiting Plaza Mayor. Plaza Mayor offers a spectacular experience in the centre of Segovia, whether you're people-watching, attending an event, or just taking in the bustling environment.

Museums and Art Galleries

Numerous museums and galleries can be found in Segovia, and they present a wide variety of exhibits that highlight the city's rich history, artistic legacy, and cultural heritage. Here are some prominent galleries and museums in Segovia:

1. **The Casa del Sol,** a stunning Renaissance castle where the Museo de Segovia is housed, is home to a variety of archaeological treasures, works of fine art, and historical collections. The museum offers a thorough overview of

Segovia's cultural legacy, covering everything from Roman sculptures and mediaeval items to religious art and local crafts.

2. **Casa-Museo de Antonio Machado:** This museum is devoted to the well-known Spanish poet Antonio Machado and is situated in the home where he resided while he was a resident of Segovia. It allows visitors to learn more about the life and works of this literary figure by showcasing personal items, manuscripts, and memorabilia related to Machado.

3. The Museo Zuloaga houses an extraordinary collection of works by renowned Spanish painter Ignacio Zuloaga and his family. It is located in the hamlet of Pedraza, not far from Segovia. The museum features Zuloaga's creations in addition to those

of other late 19th- and early 20th-century Spanish artists.

4. The acclaimed Spanish abstract expressionist artist Esteban Vicente is honoured at the Museum of Contemporary Art Esteban Vicente, which is housed in the former Santa Cruz la Real Convent.

   Vicente's paintings, sculptures, and graphic works are on display in the museum as part of a permanent collection, providing insights into his development as an artist.

5. **Artillery Museum**: Located inside Segovia's Alcázar, this museum features a sizable collection of historical military relics, weapons, and artillery pieces. While learning about the development of artillery warfare,

visitors can stroll through the castle's rooms.

6. The Casa de la Moneda (Mint House) museum offers a fascinating look into the world of coin manufacturing. It is housed in a renovated structure that formerly served as the Royal Mint and shows historical currency, equipment, and hands-on activities that explain the minting process.

7. La Casa de los Picos is a structure that today houses cultural events and exhibitions. It is renowned for its distinctive façade embellished with granite blocks in the shape of diamonds.

It periodically organises art exhibitions that let people admire modern artwork in a visually appealing setting.

These are only a few of the numerous galleries and museums that enrich Segovia's cultural scene. A fuller understanding of Segovia's history and cultural legacy can be gained by visiting these institutions, regardless of your interests in archaeology, history, fine arts, or contemporary art.

Parks and Gardens

There are many parks and gardens in Segovia where tourists can unwind, take in the beauty of nature, and take a break from touring the city's ancient landmarks. Here are a few of Segovia's renowned gardens and parks:

1. The calm Jardin de los Poetas (Garden of the Poets), which is close to the Alcázar, honours great Spanish poets. It

has fountains, sculptures, and rich vegetation, making it a tranquil place for a stroll or a quiet moment of thought.

2. **Parque de la Albuera**: This picturesque park gives stunning views of the Segovia skyline and the surrounding countryside. It is located along the banks of the Eresma River. It has shady spaces to unwind while taking in the area's natural beauty, walking routes, and picnic areas.

3. The large park known as Parque de la Dehesa, which lies outside of Segovia, is a well-liked location for outdoor sports. It's the perfect location for a family outing or a leisurely walk among the trees thanks to its large open spaces, playgrounds, sports facilities, and walking trails.

4. **Parque de la Florida**: This attractive park is recognized for its rose garden, fragrant flowers, and well-kept lawns. It is tucked away close to the city centre. With benches to rest on and take in the surroundings, it provides a tranquil refuge in the middle of the city.

5. On the outskirts of Segovia, there is a unique communal garden called Parque de los Huertos Familiares, where locals grow their fruits and vegetables. It's a fascinating location to see regional gardening customs and feel a connection to the soil.

6. **Gardens of the Royal Palace of La Granja de San Ildefonso**: Just outside of Segovia, the Royal Palace of La Granja de San Ildefonso is home to these lovely gardens. They have elaborate French-style gardens,

opulent fountains, statues, and lovely flowerbeds. The gardens provide a lovely environment for a stroll and the opportunity to take in the royal magnificence.

7. Sierra de Guadarrama National Park is a sizable natural reserve with stunning scenery, hiking paths, and chances for outdoor recreation. It is close by. In addition to enjoying the splendour of the surrounding nature, visitors can explore the area's forests, mountains, and lakes.

While visiting Segovia, visitors can make use of these parks and gardens as a pleasant diversion from the city's historic district and as a place to unwind and recharge. These green places offer a welcome break whether you're looking for quiet serenity, a family adventure, or a connection with the natural world.

Day Trips from Segovia

Due to its strategic location, Segovia is a great starting point for day tours to local landmarks and activities. Here are a few well-liked day-trip ideas from Segovia:

1. A must-see destination is the majestic Royal Palace of La Granja de San Ildefonso, which is just 11 kilometres (7 miles) from Segovia. The palace, often known as the "Spanish Versailles," has lavish interiors and expansive gardens with costly fountains, statues, and well maintained grounds.

2. **Pedraza**: This well-preserved mediaeval village is located around 40 kilometres (25 miles) northeast of Segovia. It has a beautiful ambience thanks to its cobblestone alleys, historic walls, and picturesque squares. The town also hosts numerous cultural

occasions all year long, such as the summer Candlelight Concerts.

3. Coca Castle is a magnificent fortification that was built in the 15th century and is situated about 50 kilometres (31 miles) southwest of Segovia. The castle provides a look into the military architecture of the Middle Ages with its towering towers, moat, and spectacular brickwork.

4. Located about 55 kilometres (34 miles) southeast of Segovia, Sepulveda is a mediaeval town renowned for its intact architecture and attractive alleyways. Sepulveda is also home to the Hoces del Rio Duratón Natural Park.

Beautiful cliffs and river gorges may be found in the neighbouring Hoces del Rio Duratón Natural Park, which is great for trekking and birdwatching.

5. **Vila**: This UNESCO World Heritage Site, which is about 70 kilometres (43 miles) west of Segovia, is well known for its extremely well-preserved mediaeval walls. The Basilica of San Vicente and the Cathedral of Vila are two of the city's magnificent Romanesque and Gothic churches.

6. **Salamanca**: An ancient university city with a plethora of architectural gems, Salamanca is located about 120 kilometres (75 miles) west of Segovia. The University of Salamanca, one of the oldest universities in Europe, and the Plaza Mayor are among the remarkable landmarks in its Old Town, which is designated by UNESCO.

These are just a handful of the numerous day trip choices that Segovia offers. There are many places around to enrich your experience in Segovia, whether you want to visit palaces, stroll through historic villages, or get lost in the beauty of nature.

EXPERIENCING SEGOVIA'S CULTURE

Festivals and Events

Segovia is a city that hosts numerous festivals and events all year long to honour its rich cultural history and traditions. Here are a few of Segovia's major celebrations and occasions:

1. Semana Santa, also known as Holy Week, is an important religious celebration in Segovia that is characterised by processions, religious rituals, and portrayals of the Passion of Christ. The solemnity of religious traditions, ornate floats, and colourful displays bring life to the streets.

2. The renowned Titirimundi International Puppet Theatre Festival, which takes place in May in Segovia,

turns the city into a mecca for puppetry. Puppeteers from all over the world come together to perform in theatres, squares, and other public spaces, mesmerising audiences with their artistic flair and originality.

3. **Hay Festival Segovia**: This occasion honours literature, the arts, and ideas and is modelled after the well-known literary festival in Hay-on-Wye. In September, it hosts several speeches, panel discussions, and cultural events with eminent authors, thinkers, and artists.

4. **Sephardic Music Festival**: This event celebrates the rich musical and cultural heritage of Sephardic Jews. It showcases the distinctive songs and customs of the Sephardic Jewish community through concerts,

workshops, and performances by musicians from all around the world.

5. Folk Segovia is an event that celebrates conventional folk music and dance. It brings together regional and international artists and offers a colourful fusion of ethnic rhythms and expressions.

6. **San Juan and San Pedro celebrations:** Held in June, these events pay homage to Segovia's patron saints, San Juan and San Pedro. A celebratory mood is created throughout the city with processions, music, traditional dances, and fireworks displays.

7. The Segovia Haydn Festival honours Joseph Haydn's compositions with a celebration of classical music. Famous musicians offer concerts and recitals

that highlight the beauty of Haydn's works.

8. The Medieval Fair, which takes place in September, transports Segovia back in time. A true sense of mediaeval life is created by the performers, craftspeople, artisans, and reenactments that line the streets.

9. **Christmas Market:** In the Plaza Mayor during the holiday season, Segovia holds a quaint Christmas market. A joyful atmosphere is created as visitors peruse the stalls selling regional specialties, decorations, and crafts made by hand.

These are only a few instances of the celebrations and activities that take place all year long in Segovia. These events give you the chance to experience the city's art, traditions, and culture while taking in the vibrant environment and friendly spirit of the neighbourhood.

Traditional Cuisine and Local Delicacies

The cuisine of Segovia is recognized for its robust flavours, filling dishes, and emphasis on regional ingredients. When discovering Segovia's culinary wonders, try these classic dishes and regional specialties:

1. **Roast Suckling Pig, or Cochinillo Asado:** This dish is famous across Segovia. Culinary pleasure is the roasted suckling pig, which is delicate and delicious with crispy skin. The food is typically prepared in wood-fired

ovens, producing a tasty and memorable meal.

2. Roast lamb, or cordero asado, is a different well-liked meat dish in Segovia. Lamb is expertly slow-roasted until the meat is delicious, soft, and melts in your mouth. It frequently comes with a side of salad and roasted potatoes.

3. Large white beans (judiones) are cooked with chorizo, pork, and vegetables in a dish called "judiones de la Granja," which is a classic Segovian cuisine. It is a warming and hearty dish that is ideal for chilly days. With crusty bread, Judiones de La Granja is frequently consumed.

4. **Ponche Segoviano**: This city gave its name to a popular dessert known as Ponche Segoviano. It is a decadent,

multi-layered cake consisting of sponge cake, marzipan, and a creamy filling. Typically, a caramelised sugar glaze and occasionally, almond garnishes are used to embellish the cake.

5. Sopa Castellana is a traditional garlic soup that is popular throughout the area. It is created with bread, paprika, a poached egg, and garlic. This hearty soup is renowned for its straightforward yet tasty ingredient mix.

6. **Marzipan**: Segovia is well-known for its marzipan, a confection made from sugar and almond paste. Marzipan manufacture has a long history in the city, and you can buy it in a variety of forms and tastes in the nearby bakeries and candy stores.

7. **Ponche de Segovia**: A classic warm punch created with a mixture of liqueurs, spices, and citrus fruits is known as Ponche de Segovia. It is frequently consumed on special occasions and gives parties a festive feel.

8. **Espárragos de Navarra (Navarra Asparagus)**: Segovia is not the only place where high-quality asparagus is grown, but the region is particularly well-known for its white Navarra asparagus. To highlight its natural qualities, this delicate and fragile vegetable is frequently served as an appetiser or in salads.

When dining in Segovia, it's also worthwhile to check out the city's tapas culture. Many restaurants and taverns offer a choice of small dishes that let you try a range of regional specialties.

The regional culinary heritage is truly reflected in Segovia's traditional cuisine and regional specialties. You can enjoy the genuine tastes and gourmet customs that make Segovian cuisine unique by indulging in these meals.

Shopping in Segovia

You can browse a range of stores and boutiques in Segovia to find one-of-a-kind goods that showcase the city's artistic legacy and craftsmanship. To enjoy some shopping in Segovia, consider the following:

1. Explore the shops in the city's heart, especially those along Plaza Mayor and Calle Real, where you may discover a variety of souvenir stores. Aqueducts in

tiny form made of porcelain, traditional Spanish fans, handcrafted jewellery, and regional handicrafts made of leather, ceramic, and textiles are just a few examples to look out for.

2. Segovia is well known for its delectable marzipan. To find marzipan in a variety of forms and tastes, head to the neighbourhood bakeries and candy stores, such as the renowned Pastelera Limón y Menta. It makes for a delightful and customary present or souvenir.

3. **Food and delicacies**: Take advantage of the chance to sample and buy regional specialties. Segovian goods including cured meats (jamón), handmade cheeses, olive oil, regional wines, and traditional sweets can be found in gourmet stores and delicatessens. You can also browse the Mercado de

Abastos, the main market, for a large variety of local goods and fresh produce.

4. Segovia boasts several antique stores and artisanal businesses where you can find one-of-a-kind artefacts and rare treasures. These stores provide a window into Segovia's cultural and historical legacy, selling everything from antique furniture and antiquities to handcrafted jewellery and artwork.

5. **Bookstores**: Readers can browse through the literary works, regional histories, and Spanish literature in the bookstores in Segovia, like La Tienda de las Especias or Librería Diagonal. These shops frequently carry a carefully picked selection of books in Spanish and English.

6. **Fashion and Accessories**: Look through the boutique stores on Calle Cervantes and Calle Judera to find chic attire, accessories, and footwear. You can choose from a variety of local and foreign brands as well as fashionable items that suit various tastes and fashion preferences.

7. **Traditional Markets**: If you're in Segovia on a market day like the monthly organic market or the weekly Tuesday market, it's worth going to experience the lively atmosphere and shop for fresh food, regional goods, crafts, and clothing.

Remember the opening hours while you browse Segovia's shops, which normally coincide with siesta times with a break in the middle of the day. Always make sure the objects you buy are of high quality and genuine, especially if you're buying artisanal crafts or trinkets.

Segovia shopping gives you the chance to support small companies, find unusual goods, and bring a bit of the city's beauty and culture home.

Nightlife and Entertainment

Although Segovia is well recognized for its extensive historical and cultural heritage, it also has a thriving nightlife with a wide range of entertainment alternatives. Here are some ideas for enjoying Segovia's nightlife and entertainment:

1. **Tapas Bars & Restaurants:** Segovia is known for its robust tapas culture, which makes it a fantastic spot to try

authentic Spanish food in a lively social setting. You may discover many bars and restaurants serving delectable tapas and a variety of drinks on Calle Real, Calle Juan Bravo, or Plaza Mayor.

2. Check out nearby places like La Cárcel_Segovia Centro de Creación, which frequently hosts live music performances, concerts, and theatre productions. Watch out for the Hay Festival Segovia schedule, which invites esteemed performers and thinkers to the city for stimulating debates and performances.

3. **Jazz & Wine Bars:** Spend an enjoyable evening sipping good wine or unwinding to the sounds of live jazz music in one of Segovia's jazz or wine bars. Popular locations with a comfortable environment and a large

assortment of wines and drinks include El Alambique and Mu Jazz.

4. Segovia's old district is a beautiful place to stroll through at night. Enjoy the beautiful ambiance as you meander leisurely through the city's lit streets and take in its architectural wonders like the Aqueduct and Alcázar. The views of the city lit up from Mirador de la Canaleja are particularly breathtaking.

5. Check the local event calendar for any cultural events and festivals taking place while you are there. Segovia frequently hosts a range of cultural events that offer enjoyment and a chance to interact with the regional arts scene, from concerts and art exhibitions to theatrical productions and movie screenings.

6. **Nighttime Views**: The viewpoint near the Alcázar or the Mirador de la Pradera de San Marcos offer a distinctive view of Segovia. These locations provide panoramic views of the city lit up at night, resulting in a magnificent atmosphere and providing an opportunity for treasured photos.

7. Segovia is not known for its nightlife culture, but if you feel like dancing and staying up late, you may find a few clubs and late-night places there. For those looking for a lively evening experience, El Pantano and El Pez Gordo are popular choices.

It's important to keep in mind that Segovia's nightlife is typically more laid-back, convivial, and centred on fine food and drink rather than intense clubbing. It is advisable to check the opening hours and make plans appropriately because most businesses close rather early in comparison to larger cities.

Segovia offers a variety of options to suit various interests and make for fun evenings while you are there, whether you prefer a buzzing tapas crawl, cultural concerts, or simply enjoying the city's nighttime beauty.

OUTDOOR ACTIVITIES AND NATURE

Hiking and Nature Trails

The region around Segovia is rich in natural beauty, making it a great place to go hiking and exploring nature paths. The following list includes hiking and natural trails close to Segovia:

1. The Sierra de Guadarrama National Park, which is north of Segovia, has several hiking paths that wind through breathtaking mountain scenery. The park offers chances for hikes of various kinds, from easy strolls to strenuous ones.

   The Purgatory Waterfall trail and the Penalara Natural Park, where you can trek to the park's highest mountain, Pealara, are two popular hiking routes.

2. **Hoces del Rio Duratón Natural Park:** Located southeast of Segovia, this park is renowned for its spectacular river canyons and a variety of bird species. Hiking along the river's edge trails will provide you with beautiful views of the cliffs and Griffon vulture nesting areas.

3. **Pinar de Valsan**: This pine forest, close to Segovia, is the ideal location for a tranquil stroll through nature. The paths meander through the forest, letting you take in the splendour of the trees, spot local species, and breathe in the fresh air.

4. Southwest of Segovia is a mountain range known as La Mujer Muerta. Numerous hiking trails are available in the area, including the well-known La Mujer Muerta Circular Trail. This walk offers expansive views of the

surrounding mountains as it leads you through a magnificent environment of granite rock formations.

5. The renowned Camino de Santiago travels through Segovia on its way to the shrine of St. James in Santiago de Compostela. You can decide to hike a portion of the Camino, taking in the beautiful scenery and the route's historical significance.

6. Explore the quaint villages and valleys close to Segovia, such as the lovely village of Pedraza or the verdant Eresma River Valley. These regions provide peaceful strolls in picturesque settings that let you take in the area's natural beauty and historic architecture.

7. It's crucial to be ready with the proper gear, enough food and water, and

appropriate attire for the weather before starting any hiking or nature route. Additionally, examine the trail's status and get any relevant information or permits from the neighbourhood government or visitor centres.

You can immerse yourself in the area's natural splendour while hiking and exploring the nearby nature paths, soaking in the stunning vistas and quiet of the outdoors.

Segovia's Surrounding Natural Park

Many natural parks surround Segovia, providing breathtaking scenery, a variety of ecologies, and opportunities for outdoor recreation. Here are some of the well-known parks close to Segovia:

1. Sierra de Guadarrama National Park is a sizable protected area that crosses the provinces of Madrid and Segovia and is situated to the north of Segovia. Numerous outdoor pursuits are available, such as hiking, mountain biking, rock climbing, and birdwatching.

   The park is renowned for its untamed forests, stunning lakes, including the well-known Laguna de Penalara, and rough mountains. A wide range of plants and animals call it home, including the Iberian ibex and golden eagles.

2. **Hoces del Rio Duratón Natural Park:** Located southeast of Segovia, the park is distinguished by its imposing cliffs, flowing river, and deep river gorges. Given that it is home to one of Europe's largest Griffon vulture colonies, the

park is a sanctuary for birdwatchers. The park's trails can be explored by visitors, they can rent kayaks and paddle along the river, or they can just take in the spectacular views from the numerous vantage points.

3. Parque Natural de las Hoces del Rio Riaza is a natural park formed by the flowing Riaza River, which forms stunning river gorges and cliffs. It is situated in the province of Segovia.

   It provides walking paths that wind around the river valley and highlight the area's unspoiled beauty. Ospreys and kingfishers are just a couple of the many bird species that call the park home.

4. The rough canyons and gorges cut by the Ro Sequillo may be found in the natural park known as Parque Natural

de las Hoces del Río Sequillo, which is located southwest of Segovia. It is a less-frequented park that offers peace and the opportunity to get close to nature. Hiking trails meander through the nearby woods and along the river, allowing visitors to explore the park.

These natural arcas close to Segovia offer chances to experience nature, take part in outdoor activities, and appreciate the richness and scenic splendour of the area.

These parks provide a lovely getaway into the natural beauties that surround Segovia, whether you're looking for adventure, relaxation, or the chance to witness wildlife.

Adventure Sports and Recreation

Outdoor enthusiasts can engage in a variety of adventure sports and leisure activities in Segovia and the neighbouring surroundings. Following are some alternatives for outdoor activities and recreation close to Segovia:

1. **Mountain biking and Hiking:** Segovia's natural parks, such as the Sierra de Guadarrama National Park, offer fantastic chances for mountain biking and hiking. Take in the spectacular vistas and get lost in nature by exploring the many trails that wind through the mountains and forests.

2. Rock climbing is possible on the granite cliffs and rock formations in Sierra de Guadarrama National Park. Climbers with experience can appreciate the difficult routes and breathtaking views. Observe safety

procedures and, if necessary, hire a licensed guide.

3. **Canyoning**: Go on an adventure in the canyons and rivers close to Segovia. Navigate tight gorges, swim through freshwater pools, and descend waterfalls all while being surrounded by breathtaking natural scenery. You can participate in canyoning safely with the assistance of trained guides.

4. **Paragliding**: Experience the exhilaration of paragliding and take in bird's-eye views of Segovia and its surroundings. Tandem flights are offered by qualified instructors, letting you fly through the air and feel what it's like to fly.

5. Riding a horse allows you to see the stunning scenery that Segovia is surrounded by. Horseback riding

excursions are available at several equestrian facilities in the area, and they range from relaxing rides through gorgeous trails to more challenging courses.

6. **Hot Air Ballooning:** Fly through the air in a hot air balloon to get a bird's-eye perspective of Segovia's famous sites and the area's natural scenery. A special and relaxing method to take in the area's splendour from above is through balloon rides.

7. **Winter sports:** The Sierra de Guadarrama National Park provides chances for winter sports like skiing and snowboarding during the winter. Popular ski areas in the region, Navacerrada, and Valdesqu, offer slopes for skiers of all abilities.

8. **Kayaking and canoeing**: Take a kayak or a canoe to explore the nearby rivers and reservoirs. Paddle through the rivers' placid waters while taking in the peace and beautiful splendour of the surroundings.

9. Prioritising safety is crucial when engaging in adventure sports or leisure activities. Especially if you're new to the sport, follow all safety precautions, dress appropriately, and think about hiring guides or instructors who are qualified.

These outdoor sports and leisure pursuits close to Segovia provide exhilarating encounters and chances to commune with nature while taking in the breathtaking scenery of the area. Segovia has a lot to offer outdoor enthusiasts, whether they're looking for a tranquil outdoor vacation or an adrenaline experience.

PRACTICAL INFORMATION

Transportation options

For getting about the city and its surroundings, Segovia provides a variety of transportation alternatives. The following are some of the typical transportation options in Segovia:

1. **Walking**: Due to its small size, Segovia is a very walkable city. The majority of the top sights, like the Aqueduct, Alcázar, and the old district, are reachable by foot. Walking around the city lets you take in its charm and find secret spots.

2. **Public Bus**: Segovia has an efficient public bus system that connects the many neighbourhoods of the city. The buses travel several routes, making it simple to get to different communities

and tourist destinations. The city's official transportation website and the bus stops both have information on the routes and schedules for each bus service.

3. **Taxis**: You can hail a taxi on the street or find one at a designated taxi stop anywhere in Segovia. Taxis are a practical means of getting around the city, particularly if you have a lot of luggage or want a door-to-door service.

4. Segovia provides bicycle rental services so that visitors can see the city on two wheels. You can rent bicycles from bike rental establishments for a few hours or the whole day. Cycling is a fantastic way to see the city at your speed and take in the scenery.

5. **Private Transportation:** You can choose private transportation options like car rentals or hiring a private driver if you would like more freedom and privacy. There are vehicle rental companies in Segovia, and having a car can make it easier to explore the local natural parks and other nearby sites.

6. It should be noted that certain portions of Segovia's historic centre are pedestrian-only zones, making private automobiles prohibited there. Utilising public transportation or parking in approved lots outside the historic centre is advised because parking might be scarce in the city core as well.

Consider the particular requirements of your itinerary and the distances you'll be travelling when organising your transportation in Segovia. Segovia and its environs can be conveniently and comfortably explored by using a combination of walking, public transit, and other choices.

Accommodation Options

A variety of lodging choices are available in Segovia to accommodate various spending limits and tastes. The following are some popular lodging options in Segovia:

1. **Hotels**: There are several hotels in Segovia, from high-end hotels to inexpensive lodgings. Hotels are frequently found in the city's core and the vicinity of Plaza Mayor, which provide easy access to the city's top attractions.

   The traditional beauty and elegance of many hotels in Segovia are combined with contemporary amenities and services.

2. **Guesthouses and Bed & Breakfasts:** Segovia offers a variety of guesthouse and bed & breakfast lodging options, especially in the city's old core. These places frequently provide a warm and welcoming ambiance together with pleasant accommodations and attentive service.

3. **Apartments and holiday rentals**: If you're going on a long trip or with a group, renting an apartment or a vacation home may be a suitable alternative. There are apartments accessible across the city, offering a setting that feels like home with features like kitchens and living areas.

4. Paradores are special lodging options in Spain that are frequently housed in

old structures or famous sites. A luxury and enjoyable stay with breathtaking city views is available at Segovia's Parador, which is housed inside the Alcázar.

5. **Rural Accommodations**: The nearby countryside offers rural accommodations if you'd prefer to stay somewhere quieter than the metropolis. These lodging choices, which offer a tranquil refuge and an opportunity to take in the area's natural beauty, include country homes, cottages, and rural hotels.

Think about things like location, amenities, and price when selecting a place to stay in Segovia. It's a good idea to make reservations in advance, especially during busy travel times or if you have certain requirements. Booking tools for hotels travel portals online, and official tourism websites can all offer details and possibilities for lodging in Segovia.

Segovia offers a wide variety of lodging options to suit different traveller interests, ensuring a relaxing and delightful stay in this enchanting city.

Safety Tips and Emergency Contacts

Visitors can feel comfortable in Segovia most of the time, but it's always a good idea to be on the safe side when travelling. Following are some safety recommendations for travellers to Segovia:

1. Being observant of your surroundings is important, especially in crowded places and tourist destinations. Watch

out for pickpockets and be aware of your possessions.

2. Use a money belt or a safe bag to carry your valuables, and stay away from flashing your pricey electronics or jewellery. Keep your passport, identification card, and other crucial papers safe, ideally in a hotel safe.

3. Use safe modes of transportation: When using taxis or automobile rentals, only use those that are legally permitted to operate. Verify the driver's information before comparing it to the information on your app while using ridesharing services.

4. **Maintain contact:** Keep a copy of crucial phone numbers and addresses, such as your lodging address, the location of the nearest emergency services, and the embassy or consulate.

Make sure your phone is charged, and keep a spare charger handy.

5. Be sure to adhere to local laws, customs, and regulations by being familiar with them. When visiting religious places or taking part in regional traditions, respect cultural standards and dress modestly.

6. Interacting with strangers should be done with caution, especially in remote or unfamiliar settings. Trust your intuition and exercise good judgement.

Contact information in case of emergency: Segovia's key contacts are listed below.

- Police: Dial 112 for emergencies.
- Emergency number 112 for medical emergencies
- Emergency line: 112 for the fire department

- Call the local police at (34-921-462-200).
- +1 921 419 000 Hospital General de Segovia

Keep in mind that having travel insurance that covers medical emergencies, trip cancellations, and lost things is always a good option. Check with your insurance company to be sure you have enough coverage before your vacation.

You can visit Segovia with ease and have a pleasant experience learning about the city's rich history and culture by observing this safety advice and being alert.

Useful Phrases and Language Tips

Knowing a few fundamental Spanish words will tremendously improve your trip to Segovia and facilitate interaction with locals. Here are some language and phrase suggestions to remember:

Greetings:

- Hello: Hola
- Good morning: Buenos días
- Good afternoon/evening: Buenas tardes
- Good night: Buenas noches

Basic Expressions:

- Thank you: Gracias
- Please: Por favor
- Excuse me: Perdón/Disculpe
- Yes: Sí
- No: No
- Sorry: Lo siento

Ordering Food and Drinks:

- I would like...: Me gustaría...
- Can I have...?: ¿Puedo tener...?
- The bill, please: La cuenta, por favor
- Do you have a menu in English?: ¿Tienen un menú en inglés?

Asking for Help:

- Where is...?: ¿Dónde está...?
- How can I get to...?: ¿Cómo puedo llegar a...?
- Can you help me?: ¿Puede ayudarme?
- I'm lost: Estoy perdido/a

Numbers:

- 1: uno
- 2: dos
- 3: tres
- 10: diez
- 100: cien

- 1000: mil

Language Advice

- Before your journey, learn a few fundamental phrases to show respect and facilitate communication.

- Say "por favor" and "gracias" when appropriate to be gracious.

- Never be hesitant to ask someone if they speak English by saying, "Habla inglés?"

- For rapid reference, think about getting a translation app or keeping a small phrasebook on you.

Remember that even if you only speak a few simple phrases, the locals will appreciate your attempt. Positive interactions can be greatly facilitated by a grin and an honest attempt at communication.

Since Spanish is Segovia's official language, having a basic understanding of it will make your trip more enjoyable and make it easier for you to get around town.

SUGGESTED ITINERARIES

One-Day Explorations

Here are a few itineraries to help you make the most of your trip if you only have one day in Segovia and are looking for one-day explorations:

Tour of Historical Highlights:

Morning:

- Visit the renowned Segovia Aqueduct, a magnificent feast of Roman engineering, to start your day.

- Discover the lovely Jewish Quarter (La Judera), with its quaint architecture and winding streets.

- Visit the Segovia Cathedral, a striking Gothic building, and climb the tower for sweeping city views.

Afternoon:

- Take a stroll to Segovia's Alcázar, a castle that seems like it belongs in a fairytale and is set on a hill. Investigate the inside and the lovely gardens.

- Enjoy a great traditional meal in one of the neighbourhood eateries while indulging in regional specialties like cordero asado (roast lamb) or cochinillo asado (roast suckling pig).

- Take a stroll to the bustling Plaza Mayor to experience the energetic energy of the city's core.

Evening:

- Visit the interesting Casa de los Picos, a structure with reliefs in the shape of pyramids.

- Take a stroll along the Paseo del Salón, a picturesque riverbank promenade that offers views of the city and its surroundings, to unwind at the end of the day.

Outdoor Adventures and Natural Parks:

Morning:

- Go to Sierra de Guadarrama National Park first thing in the morning. Pick a hiking route based on your tastes and degree of fitness. The trails surrounding Laguna de Penalara or the waterfalls at Cascada del Purgatorio are two options.

- Immerse yourself in the breathtaking natural surroundings while breathing in the crisp mountain air.

Afternoon:

- Enjoy your picnic lunch in the park's quiet surroundings.

- Consider canyoning, rock climbing, or renting a bike for an amazing mountain biking experience if you're up for more adventure.

Evening:

- Once you get back to Segovia, unwind in a neighbourhood tavern or café while sharing your outdoor experiences.

- Enjoy a great dinner while indulging in regional delights.

- Enjoy a leisurely nighttime stroll through Segovia's illuminated historic district, taking in the city's allure at night.

When arranging your one-day exploration of Segovia, keep in mind to verify the opening times and any restrictions beforehand, as well as to take into account your degree of fitness and personal preferences.

You may make the most of your time in this interesting location by taking advantage of these itineraries, which give you a taste of the city's history and natural beauty.

Weekend Getaway

Here is a suggested plan for a fantastic weekend break in Segovia if you only have a weekend to spend there.

Day 1:

Morning:

- Start your day by taking a stroll through Segovia's old town. Visit the Segovia Aqueduct to take in the magnificent architecture and intriguing history.

- Continue to the Segovia Cathedral, one of Spain's final Gothic churches. Take your time to savour the stunning stained glass windows and the delicate decorations.

Afternoon:

- Enjoy a leisurely meal in one of the neighbourhood eateries while sampling regional specialties like cordero asado (roast lamb) and cochinillo asado (roast suckling pig).

- Go to Segovia's Alcázar, a castle that looks like it belongs in a fairytale. Climb the tower for sweeping views of the city and the surroundings, or explore the inside with its sumptuously designed apartments.

Evening:

- Discover the historic structures, synagogues, and secret nooks of the Jewish Quarter (La Judera) by taking a stroll through its lovely streets.

- Enjoy a leisurely meal in a neighbourhood restaurant while indulging in more of the city's delectable food.

Day 2:

Morning:

- Visit the Sierra de Guadarrama National Park outside of Segovia, which is situated immediately to the north of the city. Spend the morning taking a picturesque hike around the park, perhaps up to the summit of Pealara or the Cascada del Purgatorio.

- Take in the fresh mountain air and revel in the breathtaking vistas as you immerse yourself in the park's natural splendour.

Afternoon:

- Once you get back to Segovia, enjoy a leisurely lunch there while sampling local delicacies or cuisine from throughout the world.

- Spend the afternoon discovering Segovia's less well-known areas like San Lorenzo and San Marcos, which provide a more genuine and local experience.

Evening:

- Visit the interesting Casa de los Picos, a structure with reliefs in the shape of pyramids. Investigate its interior to see where the School of Art and Design is located.

- Take a stroll along the Paseo del Salón, a picturesque riverbank promenade with stunning views of the city and its surroundings, to top off your weekend break.

This weekend trip enables you to enjoy the neighbouring national park's natural splendour, take in Segovia's cultural history, and take in its historical charm.

Check the opening times and any prerequisites for attractions and activities, and don't forget to sample the local cuisine and take in the distinctive atmosphere of the city.

Extended Stay Recommendation

You can immerse yourself even more fully in Segovia's culture, history, and environment if you have the chance to stay there for a long period. The following suggestions may help you make the most of your longer stay in Segovia:

1. Explore the regional cuisine:

- Learn how to make traditional Segovian meals like cochinillo asado (roast suckling pig) or judiones de La Granja (white bean stew) by enrolling in cooking classes or culinary workshops. In Segovia, there are culinary schools or local cooks who give cooking classes.

2. Cultural and linguistic immersion:

- Enrol in Spanish language classes to advance your language abilities and broaden your understanding of culture. Numerous language schools in Segovia provide instruction for students of all levels, enabling you to communicate with locals and experience the city more deeply.

3. Discover Nearby Towns & Villages:

- Visit adjacent cities and villages like Pedraza, Sepulveda, or Coca on day outings. These endearing locations include historical landmarks, beautiful scenery, and a window into local rural culture.

4. Festivals and Events to Attend:

- For festivals and cultural activities taking place during your extended stay, see the local events calendar. Throughout the year, Segovia hosts several events, such as music festivals, traditional celebrations, and cultural exhibitions. Being a part of these events offers a special perspective on regional traditions and practices.

5. Engage in Local Activities by Volunteering:

- Look for volunteer opportunities in Segovia, such as taking part in environmental efforts, neighbourhood projects, or cultural institutions. Participating in neighbourhood events not only gives you a chance to give back to the area, but it also gives you the chance to meet people and develop lasting relationships.

6. Outdoor pursuits and nature study:

- Utilise the adjacent natural parks like Sierra de Guadarrama National Park and Hoces del Rio Duratón Natural

Park for activities like biking, hiking, birdwatching, and relaxing in the tranquillity of the outdoors.

7. Join art classes and cultural workshops:

- There are lots of workshops and art programs available in Segovia, which boasts a thriving arts community. Join workshops in painting, ceramics, or photography to develop your creativity and pick up tips from regional artists.

8. Visit historical sites and museums:

- Visit the numerous historical monuments and museums of Segovia, including the Segovia Museum, the Casa-Museo de Antonio Machado, and the Segovia Royal Mint. You can learn more about the city's history and artistic legacy through these visits.

A prolonged stay in Segovia gives you the chance to fully experience the local way of life, pick up new skills, and make priceless memories. Take in the charm of the city, engage with the locals, and enjoy the relaxed pace of life in this alluring location.

INSIDER TIPS AND HIDDEN GEMS

Off-the-Beaten-Path Attractions

While Segovia is famous for its well-known attractions, there are still undiscovered treasures that are well discovered. Here are a few lesser-known sights and undiscovered gems in and near Segovia:

1. **Vera Cruz Chapel:** This modest, enigmatic chapel, which sits beyond the city walls, has an octagonal shape with Templar symbolism. It is embellished with distinctive carvings and is thought to have been constructed in the 13th century by the Knights Templar.

2. The façade of the interesting Casa de los Picos stands out for its diamond-shaped reliefs that resemble

the points of a pyramid. It presently serves as the home of the School of Art and Design, yet it is still interesting to see for its unique architectural design.

3. The San Antonio El Real Monastery, which is not far from Segovia's historic district, is frequently disregarded by tourists. Beautiful Gothic and Mudéjar buildings, as well as serene grounds, make it a pleasant retreat from the bustle of the city.

4. The old Royal Glass Factory of La Granja, which is close to the town of San Ildefonso, provides guided tours that highlight the meticulous artistry involved in making glass objects. The history of Spanish glassmaking can be discovered in this intriguing location.

5. The famed Spanish poet Antonio Machado, who lived his final years in

Segovia, is honoured in this museum, Casa-Museo Antonio Machado. His residence is now a museum that offers insights into his life and works through artefacts, documents, and exhibits.

6. **Valle de los Casos:** A massive basilica and memorial built during the Franco era, this contentious structure sits outside of Segovia. In addition to being Francisco Franco's final resting place, it pays tribute to those who lost their lives during the Spanish Civil War.

7. **Palacio de Riofrio:** This royal palace is located in the El Espinar municipality, close to Segovia, and is encircled by a lovely forest. The palace is nestled among vast grounds that are perfect for a tranquil stroll and has a museum with a sizable collection of ornamental arts.

8. Explore the quaint rural communities outside of Segovia, including Pedraza, Turgano, and Maderuelo. With their well-preserved mediaeval architecture and peaceful atmosphere, these charming villages provide a glimpse into typical rural life in Spain.

Segovia's off-the-beaten-path attractions offer a chance to uncover undiscovered treasures and distinctive facets of the area's history and culture. Explore Segovia's lesser-known gems by going beyond the famous tourist destinations.

Lesser-Known Restaurants and Cafés

Here are some suggestions for less well-known eateries in Segovia where you may sample regional cuisines and undiscovered culinary gems:

1. Restaurante José Mara is a well-known traditional Segovian eatery that is tucked away on Calle Cronista Lecea. Restaurante José Mara provides a genuine and mouthwatering eating experience and is renowned for its proficiency in roast suckling pig (cochinillo asado) and roast lamb (cordero asado).

2. While not quite well-known, Mesón de Cándido is a well-known restaurant that has been serving Segovian food since 1884. It is a quaint establishment close to the Aqueduct that serves

delicious traditional fare, including its renowned roast suckling pig.

3. **Café La Colonial:** This charming café is located close to the Cathedral in the core of the historic district. It is renowned for its handcrafted coffees, pastries, and cakes. Enjoy their specialty coffee blends while taking a restful break.

4. La Cocina de Segovia is a hidden gem providing classic Castilian cuisine that is tucked away on Calle Real. Their menu offers a selection of dishes produced with regional ingredients, such as robust meat-based dishes, stews, and soups.

5. On Calle de San Francisco, Café Bar Exedra provides a relaxed ambiance and a menu full of tapas and small plates. It's a terrific place to unwind

with a drink while sampling a range of mouthwatering tapas, like croquettes and Spanish omelettes (tortillas españolas).

6. **Restaurante El Bernardino:** This family-run business is close to the Alcázar and is renowned for its wholesome fare. In a warm and inviting atmosphere, they provide a range of food, including local delicacies and cuisine from across the world.

7. **Café-Bar Sonrisas:** This neighbourhood bar is situated on the charming Calle de los Coches in the heart of the city. Along with a variety of coffee, pastries, and light snacks, it offers a cosy and welcoming atmosphere. With a cup of coffee and something freshly baked, it's a terrific location to start the day.

It's always a good idea to check the opening times and availability of these suggestions in advance because they may change. Segovia's lesser-known eateries and cafés can provide great culinary experiences and a chance to socialise with locals while taking advantage of the city's culinary offers.

CONCLUSION

Fond Farewell to Segovia

It's normal to feel nostalgic as your time in Segovia comes to an end because of the memories you've made there. Here is my sincere farewell to Segovia:

Hello, Segovia

It's time to part ways, but not before thanking you for the priceless experiences and priceless memories you've given us. You have knitted yourself into the fabric of our hearts, from your antiquated aqueduct, which is a monument to history's grandeur, to the grandiose Alcázar, which has caught our imaginations.

We will always remember the winding lanes of your historic district, where there was a hidden tale around every bend. Your traditional cuisine's flavours enticed us as the aroma of roasting cochinillo permeated the air. Your quaint cafés and busy plazas urged us to explore and wander while your secret corners invited us to relish the simple pleasures of life.

We thank you for your warm welcome, the pleasant conversations we had with the people, and the special times we spent together. Our souls have been permanently altered by the beauty of your natural landscapes and exquisite architectural designs. We bring with us the knowledge garnered from your lengthy history and the creative inspiration derived from it.

Segovia, as we say goodbye, know that you will always be a part of our memories. We will be reminded of the enchanted moments we spent in your embrace by the echoes of your laughter and the whispering of your old stones.

I appreciate you sharing your beauty, culture, and spirit with us, Segovia. May your streets be a joy to walk down and your spirit endure, embracing those who come to enjoy your timeless beauty till we meet again.

Fondly,

[Your Name]

Final Thoughts and Recommendations

It's time to consider the experiences and cherish the memories you've made as your stay in Segovia comes to an end. Here are a few closing ideas and suggestions as you say goodbye to Segovia:

- **Accept the Slow Pace**: Segovia has a special charm that promotes a slower, more laid-back way of living. Take this attitude with you as you go about your everyday activities, allowing yourself to enjoy the small pleasures and discover moments of peace amid the bustle of life.

- **Tell Us Your Story:** Talk about Segovia with your loved ones, close friends, and other tourists. Encourage others to explore this alluring city and find its secret treasures.

- **Continue Your Education:** The information and cultural perspectives you earned while studying abroad in Segovia can continue to improve your life. To increase your knowledge and admiration of Spanish history and culture, read books, watch documentaries, or study more about it.

- Maintain contact with the people you met in Segovia by exchanging contact information or using social media to do so. These relationships may open doors to further travel or present chances for cross-cultural interaction.

- **Return Someday:** If Segovia has won your heart, think about going back at some point. There is always more to learn, and returning to this magical city can result in new insights and adventures.

Remember that you can always treasure the experiences and memories you've had in Segovia. As you continue travelling, keep the wisdom, beauty, and spirit of this wonderful city in mind while remaining open to the adventures and new places that lie ahead.

Wishing you safe travels and the presence of Segovia wherever you go.

Warm regards,

[Your Name]

Printed in Great Britain
by Amazon

27256492R00076